WEEKLY WR READER®

EARLY LEARNING LIBRARY

INVENTORS AND THEIR DISCOVERIES

The Wright Brothers
and the Airplane

by Monica L. Rausch

Reading consultant: Susan Nations, M.Ed.,
author/literacy coach/consultant
in literacy development

Science and curriculum consultant:
Debra Voege, M.A., science and math curriculum
resource teacher

Please visit our web site at: www.garethstevens.com
For a free color catalog describing Weekly Reader® Early Learning Library's list
of high-quality books, call 1-877-445-5824 (USA) or 1-800-387-3178 (Canada).
Weekly Reader® Early Learning Library's fax: (414) 336-0164.

Library of Congress Cataloging-in-Publication Data

Rausch, Monica.
   The Wright brothers and the airplane / by Monica L. Rausch.
     p. cm. — (Inventors and their discoveries)
   Includes bibliographical references and index.
   ISBN-13: 978-0-8368-7502-7 (lib. bdg.)
   ISBN-13: 978-0-8368-7733-5 (softcover)
   1. Wright, Orville, 1871-1948—Juvenile literature.   2. Wright, Wilbur, 1867-1912—
Juvenile literature.   3. Aeronautics—United States—Biography—Juvenile literature.
   4. Inventors—United States—Biography—Juvenile literature.   I. Title.
   TL540.W7R38   2007
   629.130092'2—dc22   2006029999

This edition first published in 2007 by
Weekly Reader® Early Learning Library
A Member of the WRC Media Family of Companies
330 West Olive Street, Suite 100
Milwaukee, WI 53212 USA

Editor: Dorothy L. Gibbs
Cover design and page layout: Kami Strunsee
Picture research: Sabrina Crewe

Picture credits: cover (both), title page, pp. 4, 7, 8, 11, 14, 17 The Granger Collection, New York; pp. 5, 18,
19 Library of Congress; pp. 6, 12 © Bettmann/Corbis; p. 9 © Underwood & Underwood/Corbis; pp. 15, 20
Courtesy of Special Collections and Archives, Wright State University; p. 16 © North Wind Picture Archives;
p. 21 © Corbis.

Printed in the United States of America

1 2 3 4 5 6 7 8 9 10 10 09 08 07 06

Table of Contents

**Cover: The 1903 Wright *Flyer* was the first successful
gasoline-powered flying machine.**

**Cover and title page: American inventors Orville (left)
and Wilbur Wright were aviation pioneers.**

Chapter 1
The Wrights Take Flight

A strong wind blew along the beach at Kitty Hawk, North Carolina. The date was December 17, 1903. Orville Wright faced the cold wind. He was lying on the bottom wing of the Wright *Flyer*. The *Flyer's* **engine** hummed, and the machine started to move. Orville's brother, Wilbur, ran alongside the machine.

Suddenly, the *Flyer* left the ground. It flew for twelve long seconds. The flying machine worked! Orville Wright had just made the very first flight in a heavier-than-air, engine-powered aircraft.

Orville's flight lasted twelve seconds. The *Flyer* traveled 120 feet (36.6 meters).

The Wright *Flyer* was the first flying machine that stayed in the air using its own power. It did not just use the power of the wind. Orville's flight was the first flight **controlled** by a person. The machine did not just go wherever the wind blew it.

The power for the Wright *Flyer* came from an engine. The engine used gasoline for fuel.

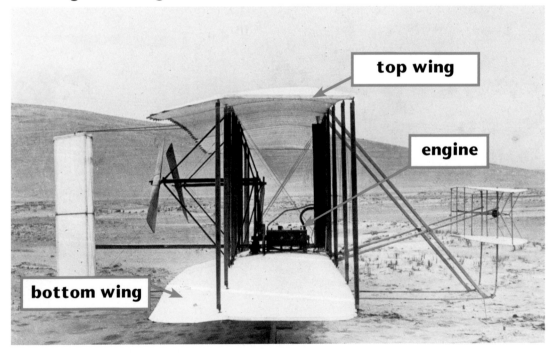

top wing

engine

bottom wing

Chapter 2
Bicycling Brothers

Orville Wright was born on August 19, 1871, in Dayton, Ohio. Wilbur was born four years earlier in Millville, Indiana. When the two brothers were growing up, their mother made toys for them. The boys liked to take the toys apart and put them back together. They also liked to fix things that were broken.

Orville and Wilbur Wright had always loved machines. They also liked working together. When Orville was twelve years old, he studied how to use a **printing press**. Later, he left high school to start a printing business. Wilbur joined him.

The Wright brothers' printing business in Dayton, Ohio, published a weekly newspaper. It was called the *West Side News.*

8

In 1893, Wilbur and Orville opened a bicycle repair shop next to their printing business.

The Wright brothers loved bicycles, too. As boys, they fixed their friends' broken bicycles. Later, they tried to make bicycles work better by changing the way they were built. By 1896, the Wrights were making their own bicycles, called Wright Cycles.

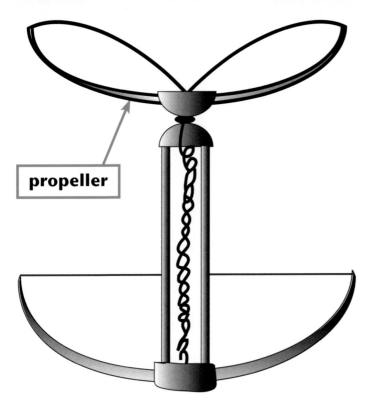

propeller

Their father once gave Wilbur and Orville a toy with a **propeller**. The toy flew like a helicopter. Orville liked to draw pictures of the toy. This drawing shows what the toy looked like.

Orville and Wilbur were curious about all kinds of machines. Remembering the flying toy **helicopter** they had when they were children, they wanted to make a much bigger machine that could fly. They wanted to make a flying machine that could carry people!

Chapter 3
Kites and Gliders

The Wrights watched how birds fly. They also read about the work of other people who were trying to build flying machines. They knew a flying machine had to make its own power so it could push itself through the air.

Unlike other people, however, the Wrights also knew that a flying machine needs to be controlled and **balanced** in the air. It has to be controlled and balanced the same way a bicycle needs to be controlled and balanced to ride it.

The Wright brothers studied the work of Otto Lilienthal, who made many gliders during the 1890s. Lilienthal flew this glider in 1893.

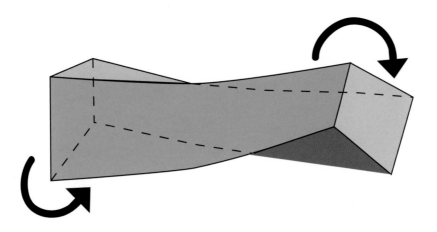

Wilbur was twisting an empty box in his hands when he discovered wing-warping.

Wilbur learned how birds balance in the air. Birds tip the back edges of their wings up and down. The brothers used a very big kite with two long wings to **experiment**. They tried to figure out how to make the wings of a kite work like a bird's wings. They discovered that a person could use wires to twist the wings of a kite. This twisting, called **wing-warping**, would turn the kite.

Flying their gliders at Kitty Hawk helped the Wright Brothers become the most experienced flyers in the world.

After flying their big kite, the Wright brothers built a glider. The glider carried a person on its bottom wing. The person controlled how the wings twisted. All the Wrights needed now was a windy place to fly their glider. The beach at Kitty Hawk, North Carolina, was very windy. It was the perfect place!

wind tunnel

In 1901, the brothers built a bigger glider, but this glider did not work as well as the first one. They went back to Dayton, Ohio, to study wings. Different shapes of wings create different amounts of **lift**, or upward movement through the air.

The Wrights built a wind tunnel to test how air flows around different shapes. They tested wings of different shapes and sizes until they found the best ones.

In 1902, Wilbur and Orville went back to Kitty Hawk with a new glider. When they tested it, Orville discovered that moving the **rudder** helped steer the glider. Wilbur discovered that connecting the wire for the rudder to the wire for the wings gave a **pilot** better control over the glider's direction.

A rudder moves back and forth to turn a plane to the left or right. When the edges of the wings bend, they make the plane bank, or tilt.

rudder

wires

wings

rudder

Chapter 4
The Wright *Flyer*

Knowing how to control a glider was an important step. Now, the Wright brothers were ready to build a glider with an engine — the first flying machine! Orville and Wilbur built a machine that had longer wings than their gliders. It was also stronger than their gliders.

The Wright brothers were the first people to discover that propellers work like rotating wings.

The machine had to be able to carry an engine, two propellers, and a pilot. The engine made the propellers turn. The Wright brothers called their new machine the Wright *Flyer*.

The brothers went back to Kitty Hawk in 1903. They were ready to fly. Wilbur tried first, on December 14, but the machine got off to a bad start. A strong wind also caused problems.

Strong winds and damage to the flying machine may have been the reasons why Wilbur Wright could not get the 1903 *Flyer* into the air on December 14.

Orville's turn came on December 17. His flight lasted only twelve seconds, but it set a record! It was the first flight carrying a person in a machine that raised itself into the air by its own power.

The brothers made three more flights in the *Flyer*. The last flight by Wilbur lasted 59 seconds, and the plane traveled 852 feet (260 m)!

By 1909, Orville Wright was teaching military students to fly. In July, 1909, a student at Fort Myer, in Virginia, completed a flight that lasted one whole hour.

The Wright brothers continued to make flying machines with more and more powerful engines. They also learned how to steer and control the machines better. Soon they were training other people to be pilots. So many people wanted to fly!

Glossary

balanced — steady and under control, with weight spread evenly

bank — to tip or tilt an aircraft so it can turn, or change direction

controlled — steered or guided by a person or a device, following certain directions or performing certain actions

experiment — (v) to try out ideas or new ways of doing things

gliders — aircraft that do not have engines and use only the wind and air currents to keep flying

helicopter — an aircraft that flies by using the power of a spinning rotor, which is a propeller-like blade attached to the top of the aircraft

military — related to a country's armed forces

pilot — a person who is specially trained to fly an airplane

propeller — an object with one or more twisted blades that force air outward when they spin

rotating — turning or spinning around a rod, or a central axis

rudder — the flat, vertical part of an airplane's tail

wind tunnel — a large round tube through which air is forced at high speeds to study how it flows around objects of different sizes and shapes

Books

First Flight: The Story of Tom Tate and the Wright Brothers.
An I Can Read Chapter Book (series). George Shea
(HarperCollins Children's Books)

The Wright Brothers: Heroes of Flight. Famous Inventors (series).
Carin T. Ford (Enslow Elementary)

The Wright Brothers Take Off. Smart About History (series).
Jon Buller and Susan Schade (Grosset & Dunlap)

Wright Brothers. Scholastic News Nonfiction Readers (series).
Lisa Wade McCormick (Children's Press)

Web Site

San Diego Air & Space Museum: Kids Page
www.aerospacemuseum.org/education/kidspage.html
Enjoy puzzles and activities on flying. Print out and color
the 1903 Wright *Flyer.*

Publisher's note to educators and parents: Our editors have carefully
reviewed this Web site to ensure that it is suitable for children. Many Web
sites change frequently, however, and we cannot guarantee that a site's future
contents will continue to meet our high standards of quality and educational
value. Be advised that children should be closely supervised whenever they
access the Internet.

Index

About the Author

Monica L. Rausch has a master's degree in creative writing from the University of Wisconsin–Milwaukee, where she is currently teaching composition, literature, and creative writing. Monica likes to write fiction, but she says sticking to the facts is fun, too. Monica lives in Milwaukee near her six nieces and nephews, to whom she loves to read books.